Are You Gambling With Your Retirement Savings?

Herbert R. Williams

THE WHY NOT THE HOW

Investing is a science. Your consultant must know the rules and principles of the strategies and products you will use. Your advisors must know all the aspects of the investment. How much you can earn? What is the risk factor? What are the tax rules. And so on.

If you go see a medical specialist, you don't tell her what to prescribe (ok well some of you might try), or what kind of physical therapy you want. **_You tell her what is wrong, what feels bad and you answer her questions._** You give her the information and let her use her expertise to tell you how she is going to fix it.

Similarly, if you go to a well known restaurant, you don't tell the chef what to prepare for you. You review the menu, listen to the specials, ask the waiter about some of the house specialties, what's fresh, etc.

Or you might explain the kind of meal you are in the mood for and let your waiter make some suggestions.

You do this because you aren't the expert. You behave this way because this is how you get the good results you're expecting.

If you could remedy your own illness, or cook yourself the most amazing meal ever, you'd stay home. You venture outside your own skill set in order to take advantage of things others do more skillfully, things for which they have garnered a reputation for doing very, very well.

My hope is that in reading this book, you won't change careers or feel that you have become an expert in beating the financial system.

I just want you to become familiar with some of the current strategies available to you for insuring you **Don't Outlive Your Money**.

Please do me and yourself a favor, and be sure to discuss the material in this book with your advisors. Then just tell them…

WHY YOU NEED IT!

They should be able to tell you how to accomplish your goals.

CONTENTS

First Printing, 2011

ISBN 978-1463636159

Printed in the United States of America

Chapter One

YOUR 401(K), IRA AND SLOT MACHINES

Slot machines are the game of choice when people go to the casino. It's probably because there is no thinking involved and it requires little to no strategy.

Are you investing without thought and strategy?

Many people saving for retirement believe that since their 401(k) and IRA retirement plans are in the market, they are securing their retirement savings.

How did stocks become the secure way of ensuring a comfortable retirement?

Like slot machines in a casino, you have little to no control of the outcome. Sure, you can pick your stocks and where your funds go, but that's the same as being able to pick which slot machine you want to play. In the end, you have no way of making that stock rise or ensuring a jackpot return.

Slot machines are typically programmed to pay out as winnings 82% to 98% of the money that is wagered by players. Meaning, you put $1 dollar in and you get $.82 back. **It's a losing proposition!**

Using the S&P 500 Index as an example of your 401(k) returns, it was reported that from 1988-2007, the S&P 500 had annualized returns of 11.81%, while investment-grade bonds returned 7.56%. But, the average mutual fund investor only experienced a rate of return of 4.48%.

If you shouldn't invest in the stock market alone, why does a 401(k) retirement plan somehow make it OK?

If I asked you, would you gamble with your retirement savings? What would you say?

Now, I'm not saying that gambling is better than putting your money in a 401(k) or IRA plan. In fact, if you have no other strategy for saving, put your money in your 401(k) and IRA. Keep doing what you are doing.

But, if you want to stop gambling on only 401(k) and IRA plans, educate yourself on how other strategies can affect your wealth. ***Don't gamble on your future.***

Chapter Two

Are Lousy CD Interest Rates Making You Sick To Your Stomach?

I'll bet they do!

To add insult to injury, not only are interest rates on CD's pitiful, but they are also subject to taxation and inflation, potentially resulting in a net loss in real dollars!

Many people have turned to the stock market as an alternative to bank accounts...only to discover that investing in the market has been very costly. Whether you are investing in stocks or in mutual funds, many Americans have seen their portfolios shrink, in some cases drastically during, the last few years. This can negatively impact your retirement plans as well as have an unsettling effect on your emotions.

According to the AARP, as a result of the market losses in the past few years:

- ✓ 59% had to change their lifestyle
- ✓ 47% had to reduce spending, and
- ✓ 34 % took fewer vacations

It gets pretty depressing. And at this time in our lives, depression should not be what we feel.

We should be enjoying our families. We should be getting that wonderful peace of mind that comes from being in complete **control.**

Feeling in control of our lives brings that peace of mind we all want so badly. And feeling like we have little or no control of our finances can make life a lot less fun.

One of the potential best ways to maintain control of your money, investing in the market's upside...and possibly avoiding the downside is a strategy called Indexing backed by highly rated insurance companies! More on that later.

Remember when you could save money at rates that would actually allow you to get ahead, and not merely survive? Imagine if time travel was possible! If someone from 20 years ago landed in this time, they would be shocked at $2.55 a gallon gas, $25,000 for an average car, the average home price being over $219,000 and the DOW over 10,000.

In the "old days", people would stay in one job for a lifetime. It was almost unheard of to switch jobs or heaven forbid, change careers!

It was common for people to put most of their savings in the local bank and their company's stock and feel secure that this nest egg would be enough for their retirement.

Think about all the things I've just mentioned, and compare them to today's post 09/11, post Enron/MCI world.

Today's world and business leaders are not believed or trusted. Politicians take polls before taking any action, and sway in the political winds, changing their minds every day. Laws are so complicated, many members of Congress admit to not reading bills before voting.

Now, things are totally different. Control is the one word you wouldn't use to describe our emotions now! It seems that a series of events over the last decade has put us all in a deep hole, really deep. And now, we're all paying for the mistakes, we're paying in the form of higher taxes, less help from the government, and with **RIDICULOUSLY LOW INTEREST RATES!**

Is it possible that some CDs are paying only 1%? Is it also possible that banks can still be charging 18% (and higher) on credit cards? (It's disgusting. They make 17% profit on your CD money.)

Herbert R. Williams

Chapter Three

THERE'S MORE RISK IN "RISKLESS" INVESTMENTS THAN YOU MAY THINK!

Let's discuss what the definition of "risk" is, in the first place?

If you look it up in the dictionary, you'll see that it is defined as "A chance of encountering a loss or harm, a hazard or danger".

Now, you'll notice it doesn't say. "loss of principal", it just is defined as "loss". This is a major distinction we need to make here.

Most investors think "risk" means that you put your investments somewhere, and the $100,000 you started with is now worth far less than $100,000. Like someone who had invested $100,000 in the stock market in 1998, and would now maybe have a value of $80,000 of the original $100,000 they started with.

And yes, this is one type of risk ...and a real one at that! But it is only one type of risk. There are others that are just as scary and that can hurt you just as badly as losing principal!

For example, if I told you that you are actually losing real money in the bank, would you believe me? Would you think I was lying, because CD's are insured by the FDIC?

A client that's either going to be, or already is, retired, will say something like, "We don't want to take any `risk' with our retirement funds! We want them to be totally safe and free of 'risk.

I guess this is the time to explain what I mean. Here's a simple example:

If you are making 2% interest on a CD, and you are in the 28% tax bracket, your net, after tax, yield is only 1.44%!

2.00% yield
x 28% tax =
0.56% lost to taxes
1.44% net after tax yield.

Now, that would be bad enough, but we cannot forget about our friend, inflation.

Yes, they claim inflation has been licked. That it's gone.

Why? Because it's been hovering around 1 - 2% for the last couple of years. Now, that is considered low, low inflation by today's standards.

Could it be that inflation has changed, or is it more likely that the government has changed the way they want us to view it?

Anyway, how does inflation affect our CD example?

Chapter Four

LOSING MONEY ON RISKLESS INVESTMENTS IS VERY REAL!

Well, remember that we're at 1.44% net, after tax yield. Now let's subtract inflation from this yield, to arrive at your true change in value, adjusted for the loss of purchasing power:

> 1.44% net, after tax yield less
> 2.00% inflation
> **(0.56%) True return**

Those brackets, by the way, mean *a* negative real rate of return! Yes, that means that you have a loss of value, $56 for each $10,000 you have invested in CD's!

Now, if I asked you to put money in an investment that was guaranteed to lose $56 for each $10,000 you invested, you'd run away from me faster than a deer from a lion. Yet, if you have CD's, then you are doing the exact same thing!

So, what does an investor do to get a better return and avoid the new higher tax on their Social Security and other income?

The real secret is to know what items you can invest in, that are off of the "tax hit list". Things like CD's and bonds get special tax treatment. So special, that they cause the maximum taxes to be paid!

What you need to do is, figure out how much monthly income you need, and then build a plan that uses tax favored strategies like Indexing to assure you get the earnings on savings you need, avoid wasting money on the taxes you don't need to pay... with assets that have some chance to keep up with inflation!

See, the risk we're talking about here is the risk of losing purchasing power!

These risks are profound, yet almost totally ignored by most investors, that is until it's too late!

This is an astounding analysis that most people do not take the trouble to understand. However, this is the most important analysis you could ever make. For what difference does it make what your gross rate of return is, when you can only keep the net real rate of return after inflation and after taxes?

Again, we are not suggesting that you shouldn't have some money in low-risk, low- return investments like CD's... What I am saying is that you must know the true net rate of return.

You must know what actually will keep money in your pocket. When all is said and done, what else matters?

Chapter Five

HOW WILL YOUR PORTFOLIO WITHSTAND A VOLATILE MARKET?

Warren Buffet, whom many consider one of the most astute investors of all time and who, through his investments, became one of the richest men in the world, says we could see another 6 to 8 years of market volatility. He could be right or wrong, but that certainly represents a question mark for the future. A "risk", if you will.

It's critical in these uncertain times to have a strategy, a plan for one's financial future. But no strategy can cover all contingencies. Even the military, perhaps the most sophisticated strategic planners, know that their plan will be interrupted when they engage the enemy. Most would agree that wars are won by the army that makes the **fewest mistakes**. The same is true in life, in the market and in one's financial planning.

So, what are the risks that confront your financial future, and how can you minimize the mistakes in dealing with them?

As we think about retirement we encounter many risks. The winners will be those who make the fewest mistakes. These risks include:

✓Interest rate
✓Inflation
✓Liquidity
✓Opportunity
✓Failure to have adequate insurance to protect your savings
✓Loss of principal, without the time to make up the difference

Chapter Six

A "MONEY MAP"

Well, the initial step, the one of most vital importance, is to have and follow a plan, or a "Money Map". There's an old saying, "If you don't know where you're going, any road will take you there!"

You see, this designing a map for your money is one of the least used, and misunderstood areas of personal finance! Most of us make decisions based on intuition, impulse, fear, listening to well meaning, but misinformed friends or relatives, etc.

It's like we're deciding to go on vacation, and just getting in the car without a map, starting to drive and make turns anywhere and everywhere! Is that any way to have a fun vacation? Will we ever end up where we want to go? Will we have any relaxation or peace just driving all over the place? Will we ever get any control of our vacation like this?

I don't think so. And, most of us never get a "Money map" in our lives. We are all driving here and there, getting nowhere.

Designing this "money map" financial plan for yourself is the secret that may change your life Forever!

I know, because over the years, I have helped many families set up and follow their "money maps" to a more restful life. A life that is under financial control.

And, I also know that without this map, people may never arrive at their destination. At least not in one piece, or in peace!

If your destination is Financial Security, you will expect to:
 ✓ Reduce worry
 ✓ Not outlive your money
 ✓ Do what you want, the way you want and when you want

It will be critical for you to know your choices before you get in the "car" especially if your Final Destination is **Financial Security.**

Chapter Seven

COMMON SENSE IS NOT SO COMMON

In the old days, good old common sense worked when picking investments. The value and potential of an investment was much easier to figure out. There was some basic business reasoning to the value placed on a stock. Nowadays, the value of a stock is much more difficult to figure out, and often has nothing to with what's going on in the real world!

The price placed on securities can go up and down like a yo-yo...without any tie to how the company is performing!

With terrorism, wars, accounting and Martha Stewart type scandals, people are waking up to the fact that the stock market is truly a very big casino, where life's savings can be lost in the blink of a terrorist's or crooked accountant's eye!

People seemed to have lost any semblance of common sense! They buy stocks in companies that lose money on every sale, and ignore solid, well run companies. Then, when one investor gets nervous, everyone starts selling and the prices of stocks plummet as if they were hot rocks. See, the real driving force behind the stock market is the emotions all of us project on it from our hearts, as well as our brains. Often, when the first group of people take action, the rest will fall just like dominoes; with pure emotion as the driving force. The reality is opposite to the supposedly, calm, cool, analytical approach many people think is involved in stock market prices.

The most misunderstood element of the stock market is that an investor's perception of general business conditions, dictate stock market price movements!

As with anything in life, it's all a matter of perception. If people perceive that things are going well, and the government has a firm grip on the country, the stock market may move up, even though the real economy is not as good as measured by economists or number crunchers.

The real facts of what the economy is doing are not the issue. It's the public perception of the economy that matters.

The perception of other peoples' views is a major factor in stock market movements. If people think that others believe the market is fine, they will jump in, which will lead to a huge band wagon effect.

We've seen a lot of this in the past decade, with people just buying into the market based on the fact that everyone else is doing it.

The same occurs with a sell-off in the market. If people hear that others are taking their money out of mutual funds, you could see them doing the same, which results in an even bigger fall in the market.

Government conditions can also lead to stock market fluctuation.

We've all seen some disturbing news about the government lead to a drop in stock market prices, even though this news doesn't really affect the performance of the companies whose price has been lowered.

We watched this happen when the Presidential election couldn't be decided right away, when the terrorists attacked us on 09/11, etc...And prices fell like they were dropped off a cliff.

Similarly, international events and conditions can lead people to buying in or selling out of the markets.

When France said it wasn't going to help the US in Operation Iraqi Freedom, for example, stock prices were affected. Even though these international events will not really affect the performance of the company whose prices have dropped as a result of the foreign incident.

Finally the media's reporting of facts or news can have a big influence on stock market prices, even though most people know that media reports are often unfounded or mere speculation.

Bottom line…

The stock market can be a very, very, very risky place to have money!

Chapter Eight

NO ONE HAS A
CRYSTAL BALL

No one has a crystal ball that can predict your
financial future.

Certainly there are a number of question marks in
your future – in everyone's future. The questions for
you are:

- ✓ Why would you want ANY question marks in
  your financial future?
- ✓ inflation protection,
- ✓ tax advantages and even
- ✓ adequate insurance protection.

For a younger person with many "working years"
left, it's easier to deal with question marks, but
frankly many retirees and persons approaching
retirement are taking more risk with their money than
they should. Why is that?

We live in a crazy world today, and the retirement
accounts of most folks are subject to unwarranted
market risk. Many say, "I'm OK, my portfolio is

balanced." But, in some cases nothing could be farther from the truth regarding the financial "safety" of their retirement!

To demonstrate the unsettled nature of the world in which we live, and its potential negative influence on that "balanced portfolio", consider the following:

- ✓ We have a huge trade deficit and a very weak Dollar - Same situation we had on that "Black Monday" in Oct. 1987!!
- ✓ Remember how the markets reacted to the bombing of that train in Spain just before their last election? Unwarranted reaction, but down, nevertheless!
- ✓ Nuclear concerns – nuke rattling in Iran, Korea and China.

So many factors outside of our control all add to a very volatile stock market and uncertainty in our financial future.

These are issues that I worry about every day when it comes to my clients and their money. If we are going to see another 6 to 8 years of volatility, and based on some projections I think that's very possible...you need to look at what happens in a volatile market and **select a financial vehicle that could reward volatility...**as opposed to penalizing you for it!

There are really only two normal ways you can buy into the stock market. One is buying an individual security. The other is using pooled funds, where lots of individuals pool their cash together, and let professionals manage the money based on whatever their philosophies or approaches are.

The most common pooled fund is a mutual fund of which there are many variations, such as taxable funds, tax-deferred funds, variable products, etc. You can also have funds inside profit sharing or pension plans, 401(k) and 403(b) plans, your IRA, and so forth.

But why buy into the market at all? Why put your hard earned money at any risk at all?

Chapter Nine

THE KEY TO
SAFETY AND SECURITY

The key to safety and security, no matter what happens with any of the variables that create volatility in the markets, is to have proper diversification!

You have to spread out the risk appropriately, so that you are as safe as possible. It's critical not to put all your eggs into one or two baskets.

Timing of your investments is another form of diversification. For example:

- ✓ You can invest money all at one time.
- ✓ Or spread the money being invested over a span of time.
- ✓ You can use investment options with different timing elements, to protect your investments.

✓ You can also invest in either individual stocks or pooled investments such as mutual funds, variable products, privately managed funds, partnerships, the list is truly endless.

All of these are elements that should be considered when diversifying your portfolio.

To illustrate this point, let me share a story with you about some clients of mine from long ago... Paul and Janice came into my office for their yearly review not too long ago.

Paul and Janice have been married for 28 years. Paul is an electronics engineer with a large corporation. Janice had been a stay at home Mom while the kids were younger, but for the last seven years has been teaching a few art classes at the local junior college.

I helped them with everything from fixing their messed up insurance, to a college savings plan for their kids.

For the purpose of this report we will only go into the investment portion of Paul and Janice's total financial plan.

Several years ago, Paul's parents died within a few months of each other and Paul was left $100,000 from his parent's estate. His parents had invested this money very conservatively in simple low rate CD's.

When they came to us we advised them about the benefits of diversifying and they agreed to go along with the following plan we developed for them.

We advised them to split the money they wanted to be in the market into some guaranteed investments, Indexed Annuities and a diversified mutual fund program. Against our advice, they wanted to buy some stocks they and their broker picked themselves.

So they put $50,000 into Indexed Annuities, and they bought a bunch of stocks.

At the end of their seventh year, the Indexed Annuities had averaged an annual compound rate of return of 11.2%, tax deferred! Their annuities grew to $105,124 in the seven years without a nickel of taxes paid!

On the other hand, the $50,000 they put into the stocks they and their broker picked, originally had done well, and the $50,000 had grown to $90,000 or so. Plus, they had to pay just shy of $10,000 in taxes, because they sold some of the early winners, and got hit with capital gains and ordinary income tax!

But, when the market tanked in 2008...they lost their rear ends! The portfolio dropped to $61,500 as of the last time we saw them. If you take the $11,500 in profit they made, less the $10,000 in taxes they wasted their net return was only $1,500 over seven years!

This compounds out to an after tax rate of return of less than 1/2 of one percent per year!

I see absolute horror stories every day of retirees, or soon to be retirees, who bought into the stock market in 1998 or 1999 and lost over half of their money as of the date of this report! Granted, those are paper losses, but they still sting and could end up being real losses if the retirees are forced to cash the stocks in because they need money!

This illustrates a point I need to make here, and that you need to consider very strongly. Here's the question you MUST ask yourself:

If I Were To Take Paper Or Actual Losses Of 10, 15, 20 Or Even 25% Out Of My Retirement Money... Would That Kill My Financial Security?

Please be brutally honest with yourself!

Try to imagine yourself needing money for retirement, and seeing that 25% or more has disappeared. Maybe for a month. Maybe forever.

See, here's an interesting mathematical equation you need to be aware of.

If you have $100,000 in stocks in the spring of 2008, and. the portfolio drops 50%, which many have, you would have $50,000 left. Right? With me so far?

OK. In order for that $50,000 to grow back to $ 100,000 ... your portfolio would have to grow 100% just to get back to break even!

See, gravity works in investments as well as on earth! It takes twice the rate of growth to overcome losses.

Let's just take a look at another example:

In the period from 1926 to 1996, investing in small company stocks returned 12.6 percent annual growth. Long-term government bonds in the same time period yielded only 5.1 percent.

So, in 1926 if you had invested ten dollars in small companies' stocks that ten dollars would be worth almost $136,000 today as opposed to only $602 if you had invested in long-term government bonds. And that's before taxes. Pretty amazing isn't it?

Now that doesn't mean you should never invest in long-term bonds or similar types of savings accounts like CD's or money markets. All it means is that in the long run, certain classes of assets perform much better than others.

There are plenty of people out there today who will tell you about the killing they made in the market overnight.

The reason these stories are so remarkable is because they are so rare. However, if you were to look at the long-range performance of the stock market the results can be no less astounding.

What if this happened to you? How would you feel knowing you had to make 100% on your money just to get even? Could you handle it?

The Practical Math Involved with Investing

Just in case the presentation of the preceding material did not make a meaningful impact on you, please consider what we like to call "The Practical Math Involved with Investing"... below.

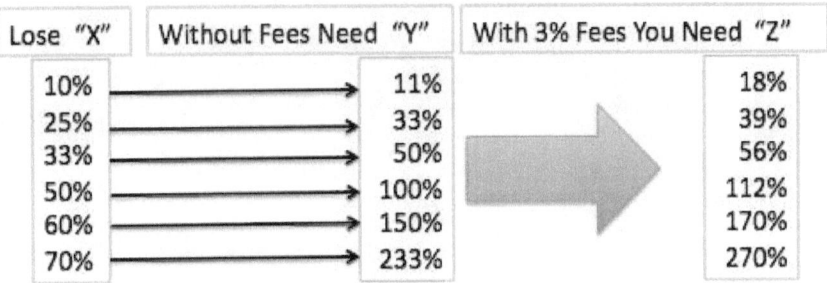

The Practical Math involved with investing: If you lose "X"% with a market sensitive investment, and you have fees of 3%, you now need an increase of "Z" just to get your money back!

Lose "X"	Without Fees Need "Y"	With 3% Fees You Need "Z"
10%	11%	18%
25%	33%	39%
33%	50%	56%
50%	100%	112%
60%	150%	170%
70%	233%	270%

This is why your chances of getting your money back can be so difficult!

If this scares you a bit, well, it should. These are very scary times, and no place for amateur night. The time of the never ending stock boom has ended. It's over.

Now I'm not saying the market won't go up, because over time, it probably will. It's just that the ridiculously easy money days are history.

Chapter Ten

THE EIGHTH WONDER OF THE WORLD

The Rule of 72

The **Rule of 72** is the most essential and simple rule of financial success. Albert Einstein (1879-1955) called **Compound Interest** "The Eighth Wonder of the World".

It will take two minutes and cost absolutely nothing to learn. Gain financial success faster after you command the power of compound interest, rather than allowing compound interest to enslave you. First we must understand *Compound Interest.*

Compound interest arises when interest is added to the principal, so that from that moment on, the interest that has been added *also itself* earns interest. This addition of interest to the principal is called *compounding*. A bank account, for example, may have its interest compounded every year: in this case, an account with $1000 initial principal and 10% interest (we should be that lucky) per year would have a balance of $1,100 at the end of the first year, $1,210 at the end of the second year, and so on.

Compound interest is powerful. It MUST be one of your financial success tools. Don't let compound interest work against you.

When you save it works for you, when you borrow it works against you.

Many financial institutions, like banks, get the upper hand by understanding the Rule of 72 and using it to their advantage.

It's vital for you to know and apply the Rule of 72 so you can make wise decisions with your savings and leverage your own financial success.

To be able to do compound interest problems in your head, the Rule of 72 gives you a lightning fast benchmark to determine how good (or not so good) a potential investment is likely to be.

The Rule of 72 says that in order to find the number of years required to double your money at a given interest rate, you can just divide a CONSTANT interest rate into 72.

For example, if you want to know how long it will take to double your money at 7.2 percent interest, divide 7.2 into 72 and get 10 years.

You can also run it backwards. If you want to double your money in 7.2 years, just divide 7.2 into 72 to find that it will require an interest rate of about 10 percent.

$$72/7.2 = 10 \text{ years to double}$$
$$7.2/72 = 10 \text{ \% interest}$$

TIME IS MONEY

Which Time Table Do You Prefer?

%	Years To Double	%	Years To Double
2%	36.00	9%	8.00
3%	24.00	10%	7.20
4%	18.00	11%	6.55
5%	14.40	12%	6.00
6%	12.00	15%	4.80
7%	10.29	20%	3.60
8%	9.00	25%	2.88

Let's say you're 30 years old and have accumulated $10,000. At different interest rates, and not taking taxes into account (we'll talk about that later) what age will you be when your money doubles?

	Annual Yield			
	2%	7.2%	10%	
$ 10,000	30	30	30	AGE
$ 20,000	66	44	37	
$ 40,000	102	58	44	
$ 80,000		72	51	
$160,000		86	59	
$320,000		100	66	

(Calculations were rounded for simplicity of examples)

Now...Your turn. Using the chart from the previous page, enter your starting amount and age:

	Annual Yield			
	____%		____%	
$_____X2	_____ Age		____	Current Age
$_____X2	_____ Age		____	Age + Yrs to double
$_____X2	_____ Age		____	Age + Yrs to double
$_____X2	_____ Age		____	Age + Yrs to double
$_____X2	_____ Age		____	Age + Yrs to double

Now let's look at the power of this rule that make financial institutions, like banks, 'King of the Hill'.

You have $10,000 you want to grow. Assume they offer you a CD (Certificate of Deposit) compounding at 3% annual interest. Using the table from page 47 you see that it will take your money *24 years to double*. You now have $20,000.

They now loan you back your $10,000 by way of a credit card. The going rate being 15% (you should be so lucky). They are doubling that same $10,000 every 5 years (rounded again for simplicity). At the end of that 10 year period they will have grown their nest egg to $20,000 or TWO TIMES what you will have made (don't forget it's taxable). A $10,000 profit on the SAME money in the SAME amount of time.

And isn't the only reason we put money in the bank so we don't lose any dollars? So, when you think about it... is the bank keeping you safe, or contributing to your losing financial ground every day?

And no, I'm not suggesting that you shouldn't have any money in the bank. No! That would be irresponsible.

But, what I am saying is that we must learn something very important to protect ourselves.

If you are suffering from these miserably low interest rates, you are a victim of loss of interest. You could be getting higher returns and insure that you won't outlive your money. You see, if you lose a dollar of interest, is that any different from losing a dollar of principal? For, after all... ***losing a dollar of anything is still losing a dollar!***

Each of us needs to become better informed regarding our alternatives, because only in this way can we retake control of our lives, our financial affairs and protect our retirement savings so as *to be as sure as possible we don't outlive our money*!!

Chapter Eleven

A LOSS IS A LOSS IS A LOSS!

LOST OPPORTUNITY COST

"The opportunity cost of using resources in a certain way is the value of what these resources could have produced if they had been used in the best alternative." *Mansfield, E., 1977, Economics, Principles, Problems, Decisions*

Opportunity costs present a continual drain on financial efficiency. It is one of the ways we transfer personal wealth to government and financial institutions. Like inflation, it is not readily visible, but compounds to huge losses over time.

An invested dollar grows, perhaps multiplies, over time. A dollar that is paid out, is idle, or is inefficient, **loses the opportunity to grow**; so, the amount it could have grown to had it been used efficiently, over any measured time period, is lost opportunity cost.

Additional costs created by how a dollar is used or invested, such as income tax, various fees, and other related expenses, are losses that are compounded by opportunity cost. Interest cost on financed items is compounded by opportunity cost.

Measuring lost opportunity cost over a specific time period is useful to analyze economic performance.

However, since that dollar will <u>never</u> be returned, the loss grows <u>forever</u>.

Losses that we would never willingly accept, had we known about them, occur routinely without our knowledge or consent.

Everyone must spend money. *The point here is to identify areas of lost opportunity cost that can be minimized, prevented, or fully <u>recovered</u>.* Here are a few examples:

Credit Cards: Carrying an average balance of $2,500 on a credit card at 10% interest creates a **lost opportunity cost of $45,236**, over 30 years, on the interest alone. This money could be in your account.

Compound Growth = Compound Tax: $10,000 invested 30 years ago, at 10% per year, grows to $174,494 today. However, at 31% federal and state, $50,993 of income tax must be paid over those years.

The lost growth (opportunity cost) caused by paying the tax is $45,171 over the 30 years. Inflation, at 3%, loses $102,602 of purchasing power over 30 years.

The real cost to achieve $174,494 is $208,766 ($10,000 investment, $50,993 taxes, **$45,171 lost opportunity cost**, $102,602 inflation).

These costs could be recovered, and the money could be in your account.

Term Life Insurance: Purdue University studies show 99.3% of term plans end without a claim, thus without value. For that 99.3%, the actual cost is the total of premiums paid, plus lost growth on the premiums paid, plus the loss of the benefit itself, which <u>won't</u> be paid. For a 35 year old, $500,000 of term carried to age 65 (at competitive premiums) has an average opportunity cost of $679,000. Even if premium payments are stopped at age 65, the cost continues to compound to $2,172,800 at age 85.

Taxes: Need I Say any more?

These costs could be recovered, and the money could be in your account.

Financial Institutions Become Wealthy At Our Expense!

However, creating a sound economic strategy will <u>reverse</u> a significant amount of our wealth transfers. Over time, recovery of thousands of dollars is easily attainable.

Having no additional out of pocket cost, "Wealth Recovery" is PURE PROFIT.

Chapter Twelve

THE TAX MAN COMETH

The discussion of Tax Deferred Investment Plans vs. Tax Advantaged Investment Plans has been an on going battle. If you listen to the media and popular financial experts, you've probably sided with them in putting your money in tax deferred investments, like 401K retirement plans, Traditional IRA, or a SEP.

Ever felt like this when speaking to an investment advisor?

"So I was in the drug store the other day, trying to get cold medication. You ever try and pick one of these out? It's not easy. It's a wall. It's an entire wall of cold medication, you stand there, you're going, "Alright, alright, alright, okay, what the hell? This is quick acting, but this is long lasting. When do I need to feel good, now or later?" It's a tough question.

~ Comedian Jerry Seinfeld

"When do I need to feel good, now or later?" That's the real question isn't it? When do you want to feel good about paying taxes, now or later? Many choose later. So, let's look at some of the misconceptions behind tax deferred investments.

What a lot of people misunderstand with tax deferred investments is that they believe they are saving taxes. This is absolutely false. There are no tax savings.

Look at 401k investments. You put money into the plan before you pay taxes. When you start distributing the cash, you pay the taxes that you had postponed. **So, with these investments, you are not saving taxes, you are just postponing the inevitable.**

Let's look at some figures to get a better picture. Let's say that you invest $1000 pre-tax over 10 years earning 6%. At the end of 10 years, your investment would have grown to $1790.85. Now, you want to access the money and you are now in a ***35%** tax bracket. So that's $1790.85 - $626.80 = $1164.05.

*Who's to say what your tax bracket will be in the future. Could be down, good chance it will be up.

On the other hand, you have another investment where you invest under the same exact conditions except that you pay taxes 35% (assuming that's your current tax rate) on the $1000 prior to investing. Your invested amount is now $650 and it will grow also for 10 years at 6%. At the end, you will have $1164.05. It's exactly the same!.

One thing is for certain, whenever you make money, **Uncle Sam will want a cut in the form of taxes.** I'd say that the probability is as high as anyone ever catching a cold.

However, there are strategies that people can put into place to decrease the effects of taxes. First, understand...

Tax the Seed

Have you heard this analogy?

If you were a farmer, would you rather tax the seed or the harvest?

Farmers would rather tax the seed. As time progresses, taxes on the harvest will dramatically erode the fruits of their labor. Remember, the longer someone lives and has their tax deferred investment plan in force, the more he/she will be paying in taxes.

Use tax-on-the-seed (tax advantaged) plans to keep the harvest for yourself.

I would never advise someone to base their money decisions solely on taxes. However, the tax impact should not be overlooked. Taking taxes into consideration must be part of your financial plan.

Whether you pay taxes now or later is up to you. The question remains, when do you want to feel good, now or later?

Is there a way I can:
- ✓ Take advantage of the tax laws?
- ✓ Guarantee I won't lose my principal regardless of market conditions?
- ✓ Have the potential for growth?
- ✓ Never outlive my income?

Are there other alternatives?   READ ON

Chapter Thirteen

---

*HEADS YOU WIN – TAILS YOU DON'T LOSE!

One of the best solutions to the dilemma of investing in the market's upside and avoiding the downside is a strategy called Indexing. Savings products issued by large, highly rated insurance companies.

You can participate in the market's upward movements and have a guaranteed return on your savings, even if the market plummets! Your money is safe and all your earnings are tax deferred. You'll never pay taxes on money you don't take out and the income you will earn doesn't cause the tax on your Social Security income to go higher!

These programs have been around a long time, but not many people would listen to us when we recommended them because in the 90's, all you had to do was buy stocks, and they went up.

But now that reality has set in about how dangerous the market is. Indexing is becoming the most popular way to invest in the market for safety of principal if the market goes down, current tax deferment on your interest, and upside gains if the market goes up!

When you think about money being in the stock market unprotected and retirement a reality you should be listening to us very closely about these savings alternatives!

The way it works can vary from company to company, but basically, you invest in an indexing contract with the insurance carrier, and they give you a choice of stock market indexes you can pick from. Or, if you want, you can use this just like a common fixed annuity, where your money gets a stated fixed, rate of interest each year, and your principal grows by that amount, tax deferred.

Once you pick the index you want to use such as the Dow, or S & P 500, etc., the insurance company will give you a portion of the growth of that index.

As an example, if you chose the S & P 500 index, and it went up that year, you'd earn a portion of that growth, which would likely be much higher than interest rates paid on savings accounts, and your earnings would be *tax deferred*!

But, if the S & P 500 index went down, *you would* earn the minimum rate in the policy, tax deferred! Do you see how awesome this is?

You get a guaranteed contract, backed by a giant insurance company, and other provisions that makes indexing a very low, low risk investment for your retirement savings.

*You get to participate in the market if it goes up. And, if the market goes down you will still earn a return instead of losing principal like everyone else in stocks and mutual funds do!

*Heads You Win – Tails You Don't Lose

Indexing is the smartest way to park some of your money you won't be touching for a while. No doubt about it.

It's very important that you know about different types of Indexing, so you'll be able to make educated decisions on where the best place to save some of your money that has to be absolutely safe from loss of principal, yet needs to grow to protect and guarantee your retirement lifestyle!

I'm not exaggerating when I say there are literally hundreds of different theories, philosophies and styles of Indexing. It would be impossible to go into them all here.

Before you make a decision, we should meet and talk about what they are and how they might fit into your personal situation.

WARNING… It's vitally important to treat your Retirement Savings as long range plans.

CHAPTER FOURTEEN

WHAT'S THE NEXT STEP?

What's right for you? Well, that's going to depend on your own unique situation. You need to consider your age, your health, your goals, objectives etc. such as:

✓ Do you need income NOW?
✓ Can you afford to wait for your investments to grow, or will you need access them shortly?
✓ What's your risk tolerance?
✓ What kind of job security do you have?
✓ What are your family circumstances?
✓ Do you have children in school?
✓ Grandchildren?
✓ Parent's that are getting up in years?

All these elements must be reviewed before you can make an educated decision. Planning like this can help you avoid unintentionally gambling with the money you intend to use for your Financial Security.

Remember..."You Can't Plan Your Future In The Future!"

Chapter Fifteen

FINDING AN ADVISOR YOU CAN TRUST

"An advisor in the Midwest once handed a kernel of corn to a farmer client and asked. 'do you expect me to believe that you could somehow magically produce row upon row, acres upon acres of corn from this little kernel?"

You and I both know you could. There is no questioning the potential of the seed. The real question would be, 'Do I believe in your competence as a farmer to grow that seed and help it multiply? Am I willing to trust you with the seed?'

Your money is no different from this seed. It has the same potential. The only question you really need to answer is, 'Do you believe in my competence as an advisor to help you manage that growth?'"

Compliments of:

We can connect at:

Herbert R. Williams

ABOUT THE AUTHOR

HERBERT R. WILLIAMS

For over 44 years retirees and those planning for retirement have turned to Herb to help guarantee their standard of living and protect their wealth. Noted for his insights, he is one of America's leading strategists on wealth creation, tax-efficient asset distribution and retirement benefit optimization.

Herb's expertise in product and strategic analysis makes him an indispensable resource when it comes to Financial, Business succession and Retirement planning.

Herb lives in Tampa, Fl with his wife of 43 years, Marsha. They have three children and three grandchildren

NOTES - This examples may not be applicable for every investor. No specific policies are being promoted in this report. Any illustrations are merely possible scenarios that could be helpful to you, and do not reflect, nor are they derived from any actual strategies. They are strictly hypothetical in nature. No representations are being made as to any future results you could experience. Your actual results will vary from those presented, and will he higher or lower than the examples shown. The illustrations and examples herein are simplified. They may or may not be similar to your situations or practical for you. There is much more information to be considered and an illustrations complying with NAIC guidelines will be provided where it is required. Please seek the advice of your accountants and lawyers. When considering investing in any indexed products, one should investigate all charges and fees usual to this form of investment. Sales charges, management fees, mortality fees and surrender penalties are often characteristic of these types of investments. Surrender penalties will typically apply. Because each of your current contracts is unique, please carefully review your contracts for all charges and expenses that may apply before making any changes. We do not give tax or legal advice. The comments regarding tax treatment in these pages simply reflect our understanding of current interpretations of tax laws as they apply to insurance company products. Since tax laws are always subject to interpretation and possible changes in the future, we recommend that you seek the course: of an attorney, accountant or other qualified tax advisor regarding insurance product taxation as it applies to your particular situation.